Guide PostgreSQL

Practical Guide

A. De Quattro

Practical Guide

1.Introduction

PostgreSQL is an open-source relational database management system with a long history of success and usage in various industries. Born in 1986 as a research project at the University of California, Berkeley, PostgreSQL has gone through several phases of development and improvement to become one of the most popular and reliable relational databases available on the market.

The history of PostgreSQL begins with the Ingres project, developed by Michael Stonebraker as a solution for managing relational databases. Over the years, the Ingres project was refined and in 1986 PostgreSQL was born, with the aim of creating a more robust and performant database management system. In the following years, PostgreSQL continued to evolve thanks to the contribution of a vast community of developers and enthusiasts, becoming a solid alternative to proprietary relational databases like Oracle and SQL Server.

One of the main advantages of using PostgreSQL lies in its open-source nature, which allows users to access the source code for free and modify it according to their needs. This collaborative development model has allowed PostgreSQL to grow and improve constantly over the years, offering users a flexible and customizable solution for managing their data.

Additionally, PostgreSQL offers a high level of security and reliability, thanks to advanced features such as support for ACID transactions (Atomicity, Consistency, Isolation, Durability) and data encryption. These features make PostgreSQL an ideal choice for mission-critical applications that require a high level of security and availability.

Another significant advantage of PostgreSQL is its scalability, which allows users to manage a large amount of data and users simultaneously without compromising system performance. With features like data replication and table partitioning, PostgreSQL allows for efficient workload distribution and ensures optimal performance even with high data volumes.

PostgreSQL represents a solid alternative to proprietary relational databases thanks to its open-source nature, security and reliability, scalability, and numerous advanced features. With a vast community of developers and enthusiasts ready to offer support and assistance, PostgreSQL remains a winning choice for anyone looking for a comprehensive and reliable solution for data management.

2. Installation of PostgreSQL

The installation of PostgreSQL is an essential process for those who want to use this powerful open-source relational database management system. PostgreSQL is known for its reliability, scalability, and ability to handle complex workloads, making it a popular choice among developers and businesses worldwide.

In this article, we will step by step explore how to install PostgreSQL on a Linux system. We will follow the installation process on Ubuntu, one of the most popular and user-friendly Linux distributions. Before getting started, it is important to ensure that you have administrator privileges to carry out the installation and have access to an internet connection to download the necessary packages.

Step 1: System Update

The first step for installing PostgreSQL on Ubuntu is to ensure that the system is up to date. Open the terminal and run the following commands:

```
```

sudo apt update

sudo apt upgrade

```
```

These commands will update the list of available packages and install any available updates for the system.

Step 2: Installation of PostgreSQL

Once the system has been updated, we are ready to install PostgreSQL. Run the following command in the terminal:

```
```

sudo apt install postgresql postgresql-contrib

```
```

This command will install the necessary packages for PostgreSQL and PostgreSQL Contrib, which includes additional extensions and useful tools for the database.

During the installation, you will be prompted to create a password for the PostgreSQL administrator user (postgres). Make sure to enter a secure password and keep it safe, as it will be needed to access the database later on.

Step 3: Verification of Installation

Once the installation is complete, you can verify that PostgreSQL is running correctly. Run the following command in the terminal:

```
```

```
sudo systemctl status postgresql
```

```
```

If PostgreSQL is running successfully, you should see an output indicating that the service is active and running.

Step 4: Connecting to the Database

To connect to the PostgreSQL database, you can use the psql command in the terminal. Run the following command to access the database with the postgres user:

```
```

```
sudo -u postgres psql
```

```
```

This method of access uses the default postgres user and allows you to access the database without having to enter the password every time. Once connected to the database, you can start creating tables, inserting data, and running SQL queries.

Step 5: Creating a User and Database

It is common practice to create a separate user and database to manage data and database access more securely. To create a new user and database, follow the steps below:

1. Creating a new user:

```
CREATE ROLE myuser WITH LOGIN
PASSWORD 'mypassword';
```

2. Creating a new database:

```
```

CREATE DATABASE mydatabase WITH OWNER myuser;

```
```

3. Granting privileges to the user on the database:

```
```

GRANT ALL PRIVILEGES ON DATABASE mydatabase TO myuser;

```
```

These commands create a new user (myuser) with a password (mypassword) and a new database (mydatabase) of which the new user is the owner. You can replace "myuser", "mypassword", and "mydatabase" with the desired values.

Step 6: Additional Configuration

Once the basic installation is complete, you can make further configurations to the PostgreSQL database according to your needs. You can modify the configuration parameters in the postgresql.conf and pg_hba.conf files, located in the PostgreSQL installation directory.

These files contain advanced configuration options for the PostgreSQL server and for controlling user access. It is advisable to refer to the official PostgreSQL documentation for a detailed guide on advanced configuration.

PostgreSQL is a powerful database management system that offers a wide range of features and advanced capabilities to handle complex workloads.

By following the steps outlined in this article, you can successfully install and configure

PostgreSQL and start using it to manage data efficiently and securely. With its scalability, reliability, and ability to handle large amounts of data, PostgreSQL is an ideal choice for developers, database administrators, and businesses looking for a powerful and flexible database solution.

3.Creating databases and tables in PostgreSQL

PostgreSQL is a powerful relational database management system that offers many advanced features for data management. Among these features is the ability to create databases and tables to efficiently and securely organize and store data.

In this article, we will see how to create a database and tables in PostgreSQL, starting from the installation of the software to creating tables with various data types and integrity constraints.

1. Installing PostgreSQL

First of all, you need to install PostgreSQL on your system. You can download the latest version of the software from the official PostgreSQL website and follow the installation instructions for your operating system.

Once the installation is complete, you can access the database using the psql command from the command line or a graphical database client such as pgAdmin or DBeaver.

2. Creating a new database

To create a new database in PostgreSQL, you can use the command CREATE DATABASE followed by the name of the database. For example, to create a database named "shop", you can use the following command:

```
```

CREATE DATABASE shop;

```
```

Once the database is created, you can access it using the \c command followed by the name of the database. For example, to access the "shop" database, you can use the following command:

```
```

\c shop

```
```

3. Creating tables

Once inside the database, you can create new tables using the CREATE TABLE command followed by the table name and column definitions. For example, to create a "products" table with columns for product ID, name, and price, you can use the following command:

```
```

```
CREATE TABLE products (

    id SERIAL PRIMARY KEY,

    name VARCHAR(50),

    price DECIMAL(10, 2)

);
```
```

In the above command, the "id" column is a primary key that is automatically incremented using the SERIAL data type, while the "name" and "price" columns are of type VARCHAR and DECIMAL respectively.

4. Defining integrity constraints

To ensure data integrity and avoid inconsistencies in the database, you can define integrity constraints on the tables. For example, you can set the "name" column as not null and unique using the following
```

command:

```
ALTER TABLE products
ADD CONSTRAINT products_name_unique
UNIQUE (name);
```

With this constraint, every value inserted in the "name" column must be unique within the table.

Furthermore, you can define foreign key constraints to establish relationships between tables. For example, to create a relationship between the "products" table and a new "categories" table, you can use the following command:

```
```

```
CREATE TABLE categories (

    id SERIAL PRIMARY KEY,

    name VARCHAR(50)

);


ALTER TABLE products

ADD COLUMN category_id INTEGER,

ADD CONSTRAINT
products_category_id_fk FOREIGN KEY
(category_id) REFERENCES categories(id);

```
```

With this command, the "category_id" column
in the "products" table is defined as a foreign
key that references the "id" column in the
"categories" table.

5. Conclusions
```

PostgreSQL offers many advanced features for data management, which can be leveraged to create efficient and secure databases.

Creating tables in PostgreSQL is a simple and flexible process that allows you to define columns with various data types and integrity constraints to ensure data consistency and reliability. With proper database design and the use of integrity constraints, you can create robust and high-performing databases that meet the application's needs.

PostgreSQL is an excellent choice for creating and managing relational databases, thanks to its reliability, flexibility, and scalability. With the advanced features offered by PostgreSQL, you can easily and securely create and manage complex databases.

4.Types of data supported by PostgreSQL

PostgreSQL is one of the most advanced and comprehensive relational databases currently available on the market. One of the features that makes it so powerful is its ability to handle a wide range of data types. In this article, we will examine the data types supported by PostgreSQL and how they are used.

The data types in PostgreSQL are divided into different categories, including numeric, string, date/time, geometric, boolean, array, and others. Each category has a series of specific data types that can be used to store and manipulate data efficiently. Let's see some examples of data types supported by PostgreSQL:

1. Numeric types:

- integer: 32-bit integers that can be positive,

negative, or null.

- bigint: 64-bit integers that can be positive, negative, or null.

- numeric: arbitrary precision decimal numbers.

- real: single precision floating-point numbers.

- double precision: double precision floating-point numbers.

These numeric data types are used to store numeric values of different types and sizes. They can be used to represent quantities, amounts, coordinates, and other numeric values.

2. String data types:

- character varying: variable-length strings.

- character: fixed-length strings.

- text: variable-length strings with greater capacity than character varying.

These data types are used to store text and character strings of different types. They can represent names, descriptors, codes, and other textual values within the database.

3. Date/time data types:

- date: date in the format YYYY-MM-DD.

- time: time in the format HH:MM:SS.

- timestamp: combined date and time in the format YYYY-MM-DD HH:MM:SS.

- interval: time interval between two dates/times.

These data types are used to store information related to dates and times. They can be used to manage birth dates, deadlines, opening and closing times, and other temporal information.

4. Geometric data types:

- point: point in a two-dimensional space.

- line: line in a two-dimensional space.

- polygon: polygon in a two-dimensional space.

- circle: circle in a two-dimensional space.

These data types are used to store geometric information such as coordinates, segments, shapes, and other geometric figures. They can be used to represent maps, graphs, layouts, and other visual information.

5. Boolean data types:

- boolean: true/false boolean value.

This data type is used to store boolean values representing logical conditions. They can be used to handle situations where decisions based on truth values are needed.

6. Array data types:

- integer[]: array of integers.

- text[]: array of strings.

- date[]: array of dates.

These data types are used to store collections of values of the same type. They can be used to manage lists, sets, vectors, and other data collections.

In addition to these data types, PostgreSQL also supports specialized data types such as XML, JSON, UUID, MAC address, and others. These data types are used to store complex structured data such as documents, unique identifiers, MAC addresses, and others.

PostgreSQL offers a wide range of data types that can be used to store and manipulate a variety of information efficiently and flexibly. With its wide range of supported data types, PostgreSQL stands out as one of the most advanced and comprehensive solutions for managing data within a relational database.

5.Basic Queries: Inserting, Updating, and Deleting Data in PostgreSQL

Basic queries, including inserting, updating, and deleting data in PostgreSQL, are essential for effective database management. PostgreSQL is an open-source relational database management system widely used for web, mobile, and enterprise application development.

In this article, we will explore in detail the basic querying operations in PostgreSQL and how to properly perform data insertion, updating, and deletion to ensure the consistency and integrity of the database.

Data Insertion in PostgreSQL

Data insertion in PostgreSQL is a common and fundamental operation that allows adding new rows or records to an existing table. To perform an insertion operation, you need to use the SQL INSERT command.

Suppose we have a table named "users" with fields such as id, name, surname, and email. To insert a new record into this table, you can use the following SQL command:

INSERT INTO users (name, surname, email) VALUES ('Mario', 'Rossi', 'mario@email.com');

This command will insert a new record into the users table with the provided values for name, surname, and email.

You can also insert multiple records simultaneously using multiple VALUES clauses:

INSERT INTO users (name, surname, email)

VALUES ('Maria', 'Verdi',
'maria@email.com'), ('Luca', 'Bianchi',
'luca@email.com');

Furthermore, you can insert data from another table using a SELECT query as the data source for insertion:

INSERT INTO users (name, surname, email)

SELECT name, surname, email

FROM customers

WHERE customer_type = 'new';

This command will insert new records into the users table using data selected from the customers table where the customer_type is "new".

Data Updating in PostgreSQL

Updating data in PostgreSQL is a very important operation that allows modifying existing values in a table. To perform an update operation, you can use the SQL UPDATE command.

Suppose you want to update the email of a user with id 1 in the users table. You can use the following SQL command:

```
UPDATE users

SET email = 'new@email.com'

WHERE id = 1;
```

This command will update the email of the user with id 1 to the specified new value.

You can also update multiple columns simultaneously using a single update statement:

UPDATE users

SET name = 'John', surname = 'Black'

WHERE id = 2;

This command will simultaneously change the name and surname of the user with id 2 to the specified new values.

You can also perform an update using a SELECT query as a criterion for the update:

UPDATE users

SET email = 'new@email.com'

WHERE id IN (SELECT id FROM customers WHERE customer_type = 'old');

This command will update the emails of users using the data selected from the customers table where the customer_type is "old".

Data Deletion in PostgreSQL

Deleting data in PostgreSQL is an operation that allows removing one or more rows from an existing table. To perform a deletion operation, you can use the SQL DELETE command.

Suppose you want to delete a user with id 3 from the users table. You can use the following SQL command:

DELETE FROM users

WHERE id = 3;

This command will delete the user with id 3 from the users table.

You can also delete all records from a table using the DELETE command without specifying any WHERE clause:

DELETE FROM users;

This command will delete all records from the users table, but it will not delete the table itself.

It is important to note that the deletion operation is irreversible, and the deleted data cannot be recovered. Before performing a deletion operation, it is essential to ensure that proper data backups have been made.

Basic queries like data insertion, updating, and deletion in PostgreSQL are fundamental operations for effective database management. Understanding how to perform these operations consistently and safely is crucial to ensuring database consistency and integrity.

By using the SQL INSERT, UPDATE, and DELETE commands, you can efficiently and safely insert, update, and delete data in PostgreSQL. Paying attention to details and ensuring proper execution of operations is important to avoid data integrity issues.

Lastly, it is essential to emphasize the importance of regularly backing up data to ensure data security and availability in case of failures or errors. By effectively managing basic queries, you can ensure efficient data management in PostgreSQL and achieve optimal performance in the open-source relational database management system.

6. Using PostgreSQL's WHERE, JOIN, GROUP BY, HAVING clauses

PostgreSQL is one of the most powerful and advanced relational databases available on the market. With its compatibility with major platforms and numerous performance management and optimization tools, PostgreSQL is a popular choice for many organizations requiring a robust and scalable database.

One of PostgreSQL's distinctive features is its ability to use clauses like WHERE, JOIN, GROUP BY, and HAVING to manipulate data within the database efficiently and precisely. In this article, we will explore how to use these clauses to execute complex queries and analyze data more thoroughly.

Using the WHERE clause

The WHERE clause is used to filter data based on certain conditions. For example, if we want to display only customers who have made a purchase over 100 euros, we can use a query like this:

```
SELECT * FROM customers
WHERE total_purchase > 100;
```

In this case, the query will only select records from the "customers" table where the value in the "total_purchase" column is greater than 100.

The WHERE clause can also be used to combine multiple logical conditions using operators like AND, OR, and NOT. For example, if we want to select only customers who have made a purchase over 100 euros and reside in Italy, we can use the following query:

```
SELECT * FROM customers

WHERE total_purchase > 100

AND country = 'Italy';
```

By using the WHERE clause, we can create highly customized queries to retrieve only the data of interest and ignore the rest.

Using the JOIN clause

The JOIN clause is used to combine data from two or more tables. In SQL, there are different types of JOINs, including INNER JOIN, LEFT JOIN, RIGHT JOIN, and FULL JOIN, each with different behavior.

For example, if we want to display customer data alongside their purchases data, we can use a query like this:

```
SELECT customers.name, purchases.product

FROM customers

INNER JOIN purchases ON customers.id = purchases.customer_id;
```

In this case, we are performing an INNER JOIN between the "customers" and "purchases" tables using the "id" column from the "customers" table and the "customer_id" column from the "purchases" table. This way, we get customer data alongside their purchases data.

Using the GROUP BY clause

The GROUP BY clause is used to group data based on certain columns. This is particularly useful when performing aggregation operations like COUNT, SUM, AVG, MAX, and MIN on grouped data.

For example, if we want to display the number of purchases made by each customer, we can use a query like this:

```
SELECT customers.name,
COUNT(purchases.id) AS num_purchases

FROM customers

INNER JOIN purchases ON customers.id =
purchases.customer_id

GROUP BY customers.name;
```

In this case, we are using the GROUP BY clause to group data based on customer names and then count the number of purchases made by each customer.

Using the HAVING clause

The HAVING clause is used to filter grouped data based on certain conditions. This is similar to the WHERE clause, but is used after the GROUP BY clause to filter grouped data.

For example, if we want to display only customers who have made more than 5 purchases, we can use a query like this:

```
SELECT customers.name,
COUNT(purchases.id) AS num_purchases
```

```
FROM customers

INNER JOIN purchases ON customers.id =
purchases.customer_id

GROUP BY customers.name

HAVING COUNT(purchases.id) > 5;

```
```

In this case, we are using the HAVING clause
to filter grouped data so that only customers
who have made more than 5 purchases are
displayed.

The WHERE, JOIN, GROUP BY, and
HAVING clauses are essential for
manipulating data in PostgreSQL effectively
and precisely. By using these clauses together,
complex queries can be created and data can
be analyzed in more detail.

With their flexibility and power, PostgreSQL
allows developers to query and manipulate
```

data efficiently, enabling them to obtain important and relevant insights for business decisions. Thanks to its numerous features and ease of use, PostgreSQL remains a popular choice among organizations worldwide for their relational database needs.

7.Using subquery in PostgreSQL

Subqueries are a powerful feature available in PostgreSQL that allows nested queries to be executed within a main query. This approach enables data extraction and manipulation in more complex and sophisticated ways compared to standard queries. Subqueries can be used in various situations, such as filtering data, comparing different tables, and obtaining more specific and detailed results.

In this article, we will delve into the use of subqueries in PostgreSQL, examining different techniques and scenarios in which they can be used to achieve accurate and efficient results.

1. Using subquery for result filtering

One of the main purposes of subqueries is to filter results based on certain criteria. For example, you can use a subquery to select only records that satisfy a specific condition. Here is an example of how you can use a subquery to retrieve only records from a table that meet a specific condition:

```
SELECT *

FROM orders

WHERE customer_id IN (SELECT customer_id FROM customers WHERE country = 'Italy');
```

In this case, the subquery is used to select only the customer_id of customers from Italy, which is then used to filter records in the orders table.

2. Using subquery for table comparisons

Subqueries can be used to compare data between different tables and obtain more detailed information. For example, you can use a subquery to compare results between two tables and retrieve only records that match the specified criteria. Here is an example of how you can use a subquery to compare data between two tables:

```
```
SELECT *

FROM products

WHERE price > (SELECT AVG(price) FROM products);

```
```

In this case, the subquery is used to calculate the average price of products in the table and compare this value with the price of each product. Only products with a price higher than the average will be returned as a result.

3. Using correlated subquery

Correlated subqueries are a special type of subquery where the inner subquery depends on the results of the outer query. This approach allows for more detailed and customized results based on specific needs. Here is an example of how you can use a correlated subquery to retrieve detailed information:

```
SELECT customer_id, order_date, (SELECT SUM(total_amount) FROM orders WHERE customer_id = customers.customer_id) AS total_spent

FROM customers;
```

In this example, the correlated subquery is used to calculate the total amount spent by each customer based on data from the orders table, which depends on the customer_id of the outer query.

4. Using nested subquery

Nested subqueries are a more advanced technique that allows for nested queries to obtain more complex results. This approach enables more detailed data comparisons and manipulations, resulting in more specific results. Here is an example of how you can use nested subqueries to obtain detailed results:

```
```

SELECT *

FROM customers

WHERE customer_id IN (

```
    SELECT customer_id

    FROM orders

    WHERE order_date > '2022-01-01'
);
```

In this case, the inner subquery is used to select customer_id of customers who placed an order after the specified date. These customer_id are then used to filter records in the customers table.

The use of subqueries in PostgreSQL is a powerful feature that allows for more detailed and accurate results compared to standard queries. Subqueries can be used in various situations, such as result filtering, table comparisons, and custom value calculations. With a proper understanding of subqueries and their different techniques, it is possible to obtain more specific and efficient results to meet the specific needs of the application.

8.Creating views in PostgreSQL

Views in PostgreSQL are a very useful tool for organizing and simplifying complex data queries. Views allow users to create a visualization of the data based on their specific requirements without having to modify the underlying data structure.

In this article, we will explore in detail how to create views in PostgreSQL, their main features, and how to effectively use them to improve query performance and simplify the work of developers and data analysts.

What is a view in PostgreSQL?

A view in PostgreSQL is a virtualized representation of a tabular data set. Views are created through a SQL query that defines which columns and rows should be displayed. Once the view is created, it can be queried as if it were a real table, without needing to know the structure of the underlying data.

Views can be used for a wide range of purposes, including:

- Simplifying complex queries: views allow users to create complex queries as a single view. This can make the SQL code simpler and more readable, as well as improve query performance.

- Hiding data complexity: views can be used to hide the complexity of the underlying data from end users, providing them with a simplified representation of the data that meets their specific requirements.

- Creating hierarchical views: views can be created hierarchically, allowing users to create a series of interconnected views to represent complex data in a structured way.

How to create a view in PostgreSQL

Creating a view in PostgreSQL is a fairly simple process. To create a view, you need to use the syntax CREATE VIEW followed by the name of the view and the SQL query that defines the view itself. For example:

```sql
CREATE VIEW customers_view AS

SELECT id, name, surname

FROM customers

WHERE status = 'active';
```

In this example, we are creating a view called `customers_view` that displays only the active customers from the `customers` database. When the view is queried, only a selection of active customers will be displayed instead of the entire database.

Views can also be created using complex queries that include joins, subqueries, and aggregations. For example:

```sql
CREATE VIEW orders_view AS
SELECT c.name, o.id, SUM(p.price) as total
FROM customers c
JOIN orders o ON c.id = o.customer_id
JOIN products p ON o.product_id = p.id
GROUP BY c.name, o.id;
```

In this example, we are creating a view called `orders_view` that shows the total orders for each customer, including the customer's name, order ID, and total price of the ordered products.

How to use views in PostgreSQL

Once created, views can be queried just like any other table in the database. For example, you can run a simple query to display data from the `customers_view`:

```sql
SELECT *
FROM customers_view;
```

This query will return only the active customers from the view instead of the entire `customers` database. Views can also be used in complex queries, joins, and subqueries to simplify SQL code and improve query performance.

Views can also be updated using the `CREATE OR REPLACE VIEW` statement. This command allows users to modify the view definition without having to delete and recreate it. For example:

```sql
CREATE OR REPLACE VIEW customers_view AS

SELECT id, name, surname, email

FROM customers

WHERE status = 'active';
```

This way, the `customers_view` will be recreated with a new definition that includes the email address of active customers.

Views are an important tool for organizing and simplifying complex queries in PostgreSQL. Views allow users to create a virtualized representation of data based on their specific requirements, without needing to know the structure of the underlying data.

9. Creating Indexes in PostgreSQL

Creating indexes in PostgreSQL is a fundamental operation to improve query performance and optimize data retrieval from a database. Indexes are tools that allow for faster search operations within a database, reducing the time needed to execute queries and improving the scalability of the system.

In this article, we will explore in detail the creation of indexes in PostgreSQL, examining the different types of indexes available, best practices for their design, and how to use them effectively to optimize database performance.

Types of Indexes in PostgreSQL

In PostgreSQL, there are several types of indexes that can be used to optimize query performance. The main types of supported indexes are:

- B-Tree Indexes: These are the most common indexes used for fast retrieval of values in string, numeric, or date columns. B-Tree indexes are balanced tree structures that allow for efficient searches using the binary search algorithm.

- Hash Indexes: These are used for fast retrieval of values in hash columns. Hash indexes are particularly useful for exact match searches, but may be less effective for partial or range searches.

- Gin Indexes: These are used for full-text search and support advanced search operations such as keyword search, phonetic search, and prefix search. Gin indexes are particularly useful for applications that require complex search operations on large volumes of text.

- GiST Indexes: These are used for spatial search and support search operations on geometric data such as points, lines, and polygons. GiST indexes are particularly useful for applications that handle spatial data and require search operations based on spatial proximity.

- BRIN Indexes: These are used to reduce the volume of data within an index, allowing for efficient management of large data volumes. BRIN indexes are particularly useful for applications that require search operations on large or partitioned tables.

Designing Indexes in PostgreSQL

To design and create effective indexes in PostgreSQL, it is important to follow some best practices to maximize database performance. Here are some tips to keep in mind when designing indexes:

- Identify key search columns: Identify columns on which frequent search operations are performed and create indexes on these columns to improve query performance.

- Avoid creating unnecessary indexes: Create only the indexes necessary to support the most frequent queries and avoid creating unnecessary indexes that could slow down database performance.

- Consider the database workload: Evaluate the workload of the database and create indexes based on the most frequent and performance-critical search operations for the system.

- Monitor index performance: Regularly monitor index performance and make any optimizations or changes to improve database performance over time.

Creating Indexes in PostgreSQL

Creating indexes in PostgreSQL is a relatively simple operation that can be performed using the CREATE INDEX command. To create a new index in PostgreSQL, you need to specify the index name, the reference table, the columns on which to create the index, and the type of index to use. Here is an example syntax for creating a B-Tree index in PostgreSQL:

CREATE INDEX idx_name ON table_name (column1, column2);

In the example above, idx_name is the name of the index to create, table_name is the name of the reference table, and column1 and column2 are the columns on which to create the index. You can also specify other options during index creation, such as the column sorting mode and the algorithm type to use for index creation.

Using Indexes in PostgreSQL

Once indexes are created in PostgreSQL, it is important to use them correctly to optimize query performance and improve data retrieval from a database. Here are some tips for using indexes effectively:

- Use indexes in queries: Ensure that queries leverage available indexes to speed up search operations and reduce query execution time.

- Monitor query performance: Regularly monitor query performance to identify any inefficiencies or slowdowns and make any optimizations to indexes to improve database performance over time.

- Optimize indexes: Monitor index performance and make any optimizations such as index recreation, statistic updates, or query optimization to improve system performance.

Creating indexes in PostgreSQL is a fundamental operation to optimize database performance and improve data retrieval from a relational database management system. By leveraging the different types of indexes available in PostgreSQL and following best practices for index design and usage, it is possible to significantly improve query performance and database scalability.

To achieve maximum performance from the system, it is important to regularly monitor index performance, make any optimizations and updates to indexing structures, and ensure that queries leverage available indexes to speed up search operations. By following these guidelines and best practices for creating indexes in PostgreSQL, it is possible to maximize database performance and optimize data retrieval from a relational database management system.

10. Query Optimization and Performance Analysis in PostgreSQL

In the world of database management, query optimization and performance analysis play a key role in ensuring that a relational database like PostgreSQL operates efficiently. Queries are the means through which users can retrieve information from or perform operations on the database such as updating, deleting, or inserting data. The efficiency of queries depends on various factors such as the database structure, table indexing, and query complexity. In this article, we will explore best practices for optimizing queries and analyzing performance in PostgreSQL.

One of the first things to consider when optimizing queries in PostgreSQL is the design of the database itself. A well-designed database with properly structured tables and optimized relationships can significantly reduce query execution time. For example, it is important to use primary and foreign keys to ensure quick access to related data. Additionally, it is advisable to avoid denormalization and keep tables as lean as possible to minimize query complexity.

Another crucial aspect of optimizing queries in PostgreSQL is table indexing. Indexing is essential for speeding up searches in databases, allowing the database engine to quickly locate the desired rows. It is important to create indexes judiciously, taking into account the most frequent queries and data access patterns. Creating too many indexes is not recommended as it could slow down data insertion and update operations. It is advisable to use the tools provided by PostgreSQL to analyze index usage and monitor database performance.

Another recommended practice for optimizing queries in PostgreSQL is using optimized SQL statements. It is important to write efficient queries, avoiding subqueries, costly joins, and unnecessary sorting operations. It is advisable to use aggregate functions and GROUP BY clauses judiciously to avoid redundant calculations and reduce query complexity. Additionally, it is important to limit the number of columns returned by queries to minimize data traffic between the server and client.

Another aspect to consider when optimizing queries in PostgreSQL is the query execution plan cache. PostgreSQL uses a cache system to store query execution plans to avoid having to continuously recompile and recalculate the most frequent queries. It is important to monitor and optimize the query execution plan cache to ensure that queries are executed as efficiently as possible.

To analyze PostgreSQL performance, it is advisable to use monitoring and query profiling tools. PostgreSQL provides various tools for analyzing database performance, including the EXPLAIN ANALYZE command, which displays the query execution plan and the time taken to execute it. It is important to use these tools to identify and optimize the slowest queries to improve overall database performance.

Finally, it is important to remember that query optimization and performance analysis in PostgreSQL is an ongoing process. It is crucial to constantly monitor database performance, identify and resolve any inefficiencies, and regularly update indexing and queries to ensure the database operates efficiently. With the right practices and tools, it is possible to optimize queries and analyze performance in PostgreSQL to ensure the database meets the needs of users quickly and efficiently.

11.Transaction Management in PostgreSQL

Transaction management in PostgreSQL is a crucial aspect to ensure data integrity and database consistency. When working with a relational database, it is important to make sure that transactions are executed correctly and any errors are handled appropriately.

In this article, we will examine in detail how transactions work in PostgreSQL and how they can be effectively managed to ensure the security and reliability of the data.

What is a transaction?

Before delving into the details of transaction management in PostgreSQL, it is important to understand what is meant by a transaction in a relational database. A transaction is a set of operations that must be executed as a single atomic unit, meaning indivisibly. This means that all operations within a transaction must be executed correctly and consistently, otherwise the transaction must be rolled back and the changes made must be discarded.

The concept of a transaction is fundamental to ensure data consistency within a relational database. Without proper transaction management, situations may arise where data is modified incompletely or inconsistently, compromising the integrity of the database.

In PostgreSQL, transactions are managed using the concepts of commit and rollback. The COMMIT command is used to confirm a transaction and make the changes to the data permanent, while the ROLLBACK command is used to roll back a transaction and discard the changes made.

How do transactions work in PostgreSQL?

In PostgreSQL, a transaction automatically begins when a new connection session to the database is started. Each operation performed within a session is treated as part of a transaction, unless specified otherwise using the BEGIN TRANSACTION command.

When a series of operations are performed within a transaction, the COMMIT command can be used to confirm the changes made to the data and make them permanent in the database. Once the COMMIT command is executed, the changes become visible to all other sessions accessing the database.

If errors or issues occur during the execution of a transaction, the ROLLBACK command can be utilized to roll back the changes made and restore the database to its original state. The ROLLBACK command cancels all operations performed within the transaction and restores the previous state of the changes.

It is important to note that PostgreSQL also supports implicit transactions, meaning transactions that are automatically started when individual SQL commands are executed. For example, if an INSERT or UPDATE statement is executed without explicitly specifying the BEGIN TRANSACTION command, PostgreSQL will automatically start a transaction to handle the operation.

How to manage transactions in PostgreSQL?

To effectively manage transactions in PostgreSQL, it is important to follow some guidelines and best practices. Below are some tips to ensure the security and reliability of transactions in the database:

1. Use the BEGIN TRANSACTION command to start a new transaction and the COMMIT command to confirm the changes made to the data. Make sure to commit only when certain that all operations have been

executed correctly and data is consistent.

2. Use the ROLLBACK command to roll back a transaction in case of errors or issues during operations. Ensure to properly handle exceptions and errors within the transaction to avoid data inconsistency situations.

3. Use transaction locking to ensure data integrity and prevent concurrency conflicts. PostgreSQL supports various transaction isolation levels, such as READ COMMITTED and SERIALIZABLE, which allow controlling how transactions read and write data in the database.

4. Monitor active transactions and their status using the system views provided by PostgreSQL. Queries like pg_stat_activity and pg_locks can be used to view information on ongoing transactions and identify any performance or data locking issues.

5. Pay attention to blocking and concurrency errors during transaction execution. It is important to properly handle deadlock situations and data locking to ensure that transactions are executed efficiently and without interruptions.

Transaction management in PostgreSQL is a fundamental aspect to ensure data integrity and consistency in a relational database. Executing transactions correctly, using COMMIT and ROLLBACK commands appropriately, is essential to maintain the security and reliability of the database.

By following the guidelines and best practices described in this article, transactions in PostgreSQL can be effectively managed to ensure that data insertion, update, and deletion operations are carried out correctly and consistently. This way, data quality and integrity in the database can be maintained, ensuring that information is always accurate and reliable for users.

12.Locking and deadlock in PostgreSQL

When it comes to database management systems, one of the crucial aspects to consider is the management of locks and deadlocks. In particular, in the context of PostgreSQL, one of the most popular open source DBMS, it is essential to understand how locks work and how to prevent deadlocks to ensure a proper management of data and transactions.

First of all, what is a lock? A lock is a mechanism that controls concurrent access to data, allowing different transactions to access data safely and consistently. Locks can be used to ensure data integrity and prevent data loss or inconsistencies during concurrent transactions.

PostgreSQL supports various types of locks, such as row locks, table locks, and database locks. Row locks are used to lock individual rows of a table, while table locks lock the entire table. Database locks, on the other hand, lock the entire database. Each lock can be set in read or write mode, depending on the type of access required.

One of the fundamental concepts to keep in mind when working with locks in PostgreSQL is transaction isolation. PostgreSQL supports different levels of isolation, such as READ COMMITTED, REPEATABLE READ, and SERIALIZABLE. Each isolation level provides a different level of protection against deadlocks and dirty reads.

Another important aspect when working with locks in PostgreSQL is deadlock management. A deadlock occurs when two or more transactions are blocked in a circular manner, meaning each transaction is waiting to acquire a lock held by another transaction. In this case, none of the transactions can proceed and the system enters a deadlock state.

To prevent deadlocks in PostgreSQL, it is important to follow some best practices. One of the most effective ways to prevent deadlocks is to acquire locks in a predetermined order, reducing the possibility of deadlock. Additionally, it is advisable to keep the lock acquisition time as short as possible to reduce the risk of deadlock. It is also important to avoid holding locks for too long and release them as soon as possible after completing the operation.

Another recommended practice to prevent deadlocks in PostgreSQL is to use short and atomic transactions. A short transaction is less susceptible to deadlocks, as it reduces the time during which locks are held. Furthermore, it is important to ensure that transactions are atomic, meaning they are executed completely and consistently, to avoid deadlock situations.

PostgreSQL also provides tools to detect and resolve deadlocks. You can monitor active locks using PostgreSQL's system commands, such as pg_locks and pg_stat_activity. Additionally, you can use the EXPLAIN command to analyze queries and identify potential deadlock situations.

Managing locks and deadlocks in PostgreSQL is a fundamental aspect to ensure proper data and transaction management. By following best practices and using the tools provided by PostgreSQL, you can prevent deadlocks and ensure effective lock management. It is important to understand the different types of locks supported by PostgreSQL and use the appropriate isolation level to protect data and prevent deadlock situations. With proper lock and deadlock management, you can ensure the security and integrity of data in the PostgreSQL database.

13.Example of PostgreSQL database

PostgreSQL is a very powerful and versatile relational database management system. It is an open-source software that offers numerous tools for data management and the creation of complex databases. In this article, I will guide you step by step through creating a sample database using PostgreSQL.

Step 1: Installing PostgreSQL

First, you need to install PostgreSQL on your system. You can do this by following the instructions on the official PostgreSQL website. Once the installation is complete, you will need to create a user and an administration password to access the database.

Step 2: Creating a database

Once PostgreSQL is installed, you can now create a database. You can do this using the createdatabase command. For example, to create a new database called "example," you can use the following command:

```
```

CREATE DATABASE example;

```
```

Step 3: Creating a table

After creating the database, you can start creating tables within it. In PostgreSQL, tables are created using the createtable command. For example, to create a table called "customers" with fields like id, name, last name, and email, you can use the following command:

```
CREATE TABLE customers (

  id SERIAL PRIMARY KEY,

  name VARCHAR(50),

  last_name VARCHAR(50),

  email VARCHAR(50)

);
```

In this example, the "id" field is of serial type, which means it will automatically increment by one each time a new record is added. The "name," "last_name," and "email" fields are of varchar type and can contain up to 50 characters each.

Step 4: Inserting data into the table

After creating the table, you can insert data

into it using the insert into command. For example, to add a new customer to the "customers" table, you can use the following command:

```
```

INSERT INTO customers (name, last_name, email) VALUES ('Mario', 'Rossi', 'mario.rossi@email.com');

```
```

This command will insert a new record into the "customers" table with the specified values for the "name," "last_name," and "email" fields.

Step 5: Querying data

Once you have inserted data into the table, you can run queries to retrieve specific information. For example, to select all customers from the "customers" table, you can use the following command:

```
SELECT * FROM customers;
```

This command will return all records in the "customers" table along with all fields.

Step 6: Updating data

You can update the data in the table using the update command. For example, to update the email of a customer with id 1, you can use the following command:

```
UPDATE customers SET
```

email='new@email.com' WHERE id=1;

```
```

This command updates the "email" field of the customer with id 1 with the specified new value.

Step 7: Deleting data

To delete data from the table, you can use the delete from command. For example, to delete a customer with id 1 from the "customers" table, you can use the following command:

```
```

DELETE FROM customers WHERE id=1;

```
```

This command will delete the record of the

customer with id 1 from the table.

Step 8: Creating relationships

In PostgreSQL, you can create relationships between tables using foreign keys. For example, if you want to create a relationship between the "customers" table and a new "orders" table, you can do so by adding a foreign key to the "orders" table that references the "customers" table.

Step 9: Backup and restore

It is important to regularly back up the database to prevent data loss. You can use the pg_dump command to back up and the pg_restore command to restore data from a previous backup.

Step 10: Database security

Finally, it is important to protect the database from unauthorized access. This can be done by setting up complex passwords for user accounts and limiting database access using permissions.

PostgreSQL is a very powerful and flexible database management system that offers numerous features for creating and managing databases. By following the steps mentioned above, you can effectively utilize PostgreSQL for your database needs.

14. Data Recovery in PostgreSQL

Data recovery in PostgreSQL is a fundamental process to ensure the security and integrity of data within a database. There are several methods and tools that allow you to perform data recovery in PostgreSQL, each with its own characteristics and advantages.

In this guide, we will delve into the key aspects related to data recovery in PostgreSQL, providing practical guidance on how to perform this operation effectively and securely.

Definition of data recovery in PostgreSQL

Data recovery in PostgreSQL involves restoring a database or specific tables from a previously made backup. This process is essential for recovering data in case of loss or damage to the database, such as due to human error, hardware malfunction, or a cyber-attack.

There are different types of backups that can be made in PostgreSQL, each with its own characteristics and restoration methods:

- Physical backup: involves an exact copy of the data and log files of the database. Restoring a physical backup involves restoring all the data present in the database.

- Logical backup: involves a logical copy of the data within the database, usually in the form of text files containing SQL commands to recreate tables and data. Restoring a logical backup allows you to select individual tables or data to restore.

Methods for data recovery in PostgreSQL

There are various methods to perform data recovery in PostgreSQL, each with its own characteristics and usage methods:

1. pg_restore: pg_restore is the native tool in PostgreSQL for data recovery from a backup. To use pg_restore, you need to have a backup previously made with pg_dump, as pg_restore uses the file format created by pg_dump for data restoration.

To restore a backup with pg_restore, simply execute the following command from the command line:

pg_restore -d database_name -U username backup_file

where "database_name" is the name of the database where you want to restore the data, "username" is the name of the user with the necessary privileges to restore the backup, and "backup_file" is the name of the backup file to restore.

2. pg_dump: pg_dump is the native tool in PostgreSQL to make a backup of the data within a database. Using pg_dump, you can create a physical or logical backup of the data, depending on your needs.

To create a physical backup with pg_dump, you can use the following command from the command line:

pg_dump -Fc -f backup_file.dump database_name

where "-Fc" indicates that the backup should be created in custom format, "-f" specifies the name of the backup file to create, and "database_name" is the name of the database from which to backup.

3. Backup and restore via psql: you can

perform backup and data recovery directly through the PostgreSQL client psql, using shell commands "\copy" and "\i".

To export data from a table to a text file, you can use the following command:

\copy table_name TO 'file_name.txt'

To import data from a text file into a table, you can use the following command:

\copy table_name FROM 'file_name.txt'

These are just some of the most common methods to perform data recovery in PostgreSQL. It is important to assess your needs and choose the most suitable method based on the specific characteristics of your database.

Best practices for data recovery in PostgreSQL

To ensure effective and secure data recovery in PostgreSQL, it is important to follow some best practices:

1. Regular backups: it is essential to make regular backups of the data within the database so that you can recover the data in case of loss or damage to the database.

2. Test backups: it is advisable to regularly test backups to verify that they are correctly created and can be successfully restored when needed.

3. Monitor restoration processes: it is important to closely monitor data recovery processes to detect any errors or issues and

intervene promptly.

4. Use backup versioning: it is advisable to use a backup versioning strategy so that you can recover data from previous versions of the database if needed.

5. Keep software and security patches up to date: it is important to keep software and security patches up to date to ensure the protection of data within the database from potential external threats.

Data recovery in PostgreSQL is a fundamental process to ensure the security and integrity of data within a database. There are several methods and tools that allow you to perform data recovery effectively and securely, each with its own characteristics and advantages.

Following best practices for data recovery in PostgreSQL is essential to ensure data protection and operational continuity of the database. With proper planning and attention to detail, you can perform data recovery efficiently and safely, ensuring the availability and integrity of information within the database.

With proper planning and attention to detail, you can perform data recovery efficiently and safely, ensuring the availability and integrity of information within the database.

15. Backup and Restore of Databases in PostgreSQL

Backup and restore of databases are essential to ensure the security and reliability of data in a database management system like PostgreSQL. In this article, we will explore best practices for performing backup and restore of databases in PostgreSQL, as well as the various options available to implement an effective backup system.

Backup of a PostgreSQL database

Backing up a PostgreSQL database can be done in various ways, including physical and logical backups. A physical backup of a PostgreSQL database involves copying the database's data files directly from the filesystem, while a logical backup involves exporting the data in SQL format.

A common way to perform a physical backup of a PostgreSQL database is to use the pg_dumpall command to export all databases in their current state. This command creates a dump of all databases in SQL format that can be used to restore data if needed.

Here is an example of how to use the pg_dumpall command to perform a physical backup of a PostgreSQL database:

```
$ pg_dumpall > backup.sql
```

This command dumps all databases in the system into a file named backup.sql. This file can be used to restore data in case of loss or corruption of the original database.

Another common method to perform a physical backup of a single PostgreSQL database is to use the pg_dump command to export the database in SQL format. For example, to back up the "mydatabase" database, you can use the following command:

```
$ pg_dump mydatabase > mydatabase_backup.sql
```

This command will create a dump of the "mydatabase" database into a file named mydatabase_backup.sql that can be used to restore the database if needed.

In addition to physical backup, a logical backup of a PostgreSQL database can be done using the pg_dump command to export data in SQL format. Again, you can back up all databases at once using the pg_dumpall command or back up a single database using the pg_dump command.

It is important to note that logical backup may be slower and require more resources than physical backup, as it involves the process of exporting data in SQL format. However, logical backup offers the flexibility to export individual databases or tables, which can be useful in certain scenarios.

Restore of a PostgreSQL database

Restoring a PostgreSQL database can be done using the dump created during the backup. To restore a PostgreSQL database from a dump file, you can use the psql command to execute the dump into the desired database.

For example, to restore a database from a dump file created with the pg_dump command, you can use the following command:

```
$ psql -d mydatabase -f
mydatabase_backup.sql
```

This command will restore the "mydatabase" database from the dump file mydatabase_backup.sql. Once the restore process is complete, the database will be returned to the state it was in at the time of the backup.

It is important to note that restoring a PostgreSQL database will overwrite existing data in the database. Before performing the restore, it is advisable to back up existing data to prevent the loss of important information.

Advanced options for backup and restore

In addition to the standard backup and restore methods described above, PostgreSQL offers several advanced options to implement a more sophisticated and reliable backup and restore system.

One of these options is hot standby

replication, which involves creating a real-time replica of the database on a backup server. With hot standby replication, you can restore the database much more quickly than traditional backup and restore methods, as the backup server is already synchronized with the primary database.

Another advanced option for backup and restore is point-in-time recovery, which allows you to restore a PostgreSQL database to a specific state at a specific time. This option is particularly useful in case of errors or malfunctions that require restoring data to a previous state.

Backup and restore of databases are essential to ensure the security and reliability of data in a database management system like PostgreSQL. In today's article, we have explored best practices for performing backup and restore of databases in PostgreSQL, as well as the various options available to implement an effective backup system.

Regardless of the method chosen to perform backup and restore of databases in PostgreSQL, it is important to regularly test the backup and restore processes to ensure that data can be successfully restored if needed. With the right practices and procedures in place, you can ensure the security and integrity of data and mitigate the risks of losing valuable information.

16.Backup and restore of individual tables in PostgreSQL

PostgreSQL is one of the most popular open-source databases in the world, with a wide range of advanced features and an active community of users and developers. One of the most important features of PostgreSQL is its robust backup and data restoration management capabilities, allowing users to protect their critical information from accidental loss or damage.

In this article, we will examine in detail how to back up and restore individual tables in PostgreSQL, an operation useful for efficiently managing data without having to create backup copies of the entire database. We will follow detailed steps to back up a single table, restore the backup, and restore only specific parts of the table.

Backing up a single table in PostgreSQL

Backing up a single table in PostgreSQL can be useful when you want to preserve only a portion of the data without creating a complete backup of the database. Here are the steps to back up a single table in PostgreSQL:

Connect to the database: First, connect to the PostgreSQL database where the table you want to back up is located. Use the psql command or a database administration tool to access the database.

Execute the dump command: Use the pg_dump command to back up the desired table. For example, to back up the "users" table in the "mydb" database, execute the following command:

pg_dump -d mydb -t users > backup_users.sql

This command dumps only the "users" table in the "mydb" database and saves it in the backup file "backup_users.sql".

Verify the backup file: After executing the dump command, verify that the backup file has been created correctly. Use the ls command to list the files in the current directory and verify that the backup file is present.

Conclusion of the backup: Once the backup file has been created, the backup of the single table in PostgreSQL is complete. The backup file can be stored in a secure location or transferred to another server for restoration.

Restoring a single table in PostgreSQL

After backing up a single table in PostgreSQL, you can restore it in case of data loss or issues in the database. Here are the steps to restore a single table in PostgreSQL:

Connect to the database: Before restoring the table, connect to the PostgreSQL database where you want to restore the data. Once again, use the psql command or a database administration tool to access the database.

Execute the restore command: Use the psql command to restore the table from the backup copy. For example, to restore the "users" table from the "backup_users.sql" file in the "mydb" database, execute the following command:

```
psql -d mydb -f backup_users.sql
```

This command restores the "users" table in the "mydb" database from the "backup_users.sql" backup file.

Verify the restoration: After executing the

restore command, verify that the table has been successfully restored in the database. Execute SELECT queries to verify that the data has been restored correctly.

Conclusion of the restoration: Once the table has been successfully restored, the restoration of the single table in PostgreSQL is complete. The data is now available again in the database and can be used for routine operations.

Restoring specific parts of a table in PostgreSQL

In some cases, it may be necessary to restore only specific parts of a table in PostgreSQL, such as certain rows or columns. You can use the COPY command to load only specific parts of the table from the backup file. Here's how to restore specific parts of a table in PostgreSQL:

Create a custom backup file: Before being able to restore specific parts of a table, you need to create a custom backup file that includes only the desired parts. Use the pg_dump command with the -t option to specify the table and the -a option to include only specific rows. For example, to back up only the first 10 rows of the "users" table in the "mydb" database, execute the following command:

```
pg_dump -d mydb -t users -a -n 10 >
backup_users_custom.sql
```

This command dumps the first 10 records of the "users" table in the "mydb" database and saves it in the custom backup file "backup_users_custom.sql".

Execute the custom restore command: After creating the custom backup file, you can restore specific parts of the table using the COPY command in PostgreSQL. For example, to load only the first 10 rows from the custom backup file into the "mydb" database, execute the following command:

```
psql -d mydb -c "COPY users FROM '/path/to/backup_users_custom.sql'"
```

This command loads only the first 10 rows of the "users" table from the custom backup file into the "mydb" database.

Verify the custom restoration: After executing the custom restore command, verify that only the specific parts of the table have been restored in the database. Execute SELECT queries to verify that only the desired rows or columns have been successfully restored.

Conclusion of the custom restoration: Once the specific parts of the table have been successfully restored, the custom restoration is complete. The desired parts of the table are now available in the database and can be used for routine operations.Backing up and restoring individual tables in PostgreSQL are operations useful for protecting and efficiently managing data in the database. By following the detailed steps described in this article, you can easily and accurately back up and restore individual tables. Remember to always keep backups in a secure location and regularly check that the data has been restored correctly to ensure business operations continuity. For more information on how to back up and restore in PostgreSQL, consult the official database documentation and interact with the user and developer community for additional support and advice.

17. User and Privilege Management in PostgreSQL

User and privilege management in PostgreSQL is a crucial aspect to ensure the security and integrity of data within the database. In this guide, we will explore the main tools and techniques available to manage users and privileges in PostgreSQL, providing a comprehensive overview of best practices to follow to ensure a proper configuration of the system.

Thanks to its modular and flexible architecture, PostgreSQL offers a wide range of advanced features and management tools that allow developers to create and manage complex databases efficiently.

Among the most important features of PostgreSQL is the ability to define and manage users and privileges, which allow controlling access to data and database resources in a granular and customized way. In this article, we will examine how to use PostgreSQL tools to create and manage users, roles, and privileges efficiently and securely.

Creating a User in PostgreSQL

Before being able to manage privileges within PostgreSQL, it is necessary to create a user that can be associated with one or more roles and to whom the necessary access privileges can be assigned. To create a new user in PostgreSQL, you can use the `CREATE USER` command followed by the user's name and, optionally, the access password.

For example, to create a new user named "new_user" with an access password, you can use the following SQL command:

```sql
```

```
CREATE USER new_user WITH
PASSWORD 'password';

```
```

Once the user is created, you can assign one or more roles to them, defining the access privileges and authorizations associated with the user. Roles in PostgreSQL allow grouping a set of privileges and authorizations that can be assigned to one or more users, simplifying the management of access and permissions within the database.

Creating Roles in PostgreSQL

In addition to users, you can create roles in PostgreSQL to define a set of privileges and authorizations that can be assigned to one or more users. Roles allow efficiently organizing access privileges and authorizations within the database, simplifying the management of users and access permissions.
```

To create a new role in PostgreSQL, you can use the `CREATE ROLE` command followed by the role's name and, optionally, the list of roles that the new role is authorized to inherit. For example, to create a new role named "administrator" that inherits the privileges of the "superuser" role, you can use the following SQL command:

```sql
CREATE ROLE administrator INHERIT superuser;
```

Once the role is created, you can assign it the necessary access privileges and authorizations to manage users and data within the database. Privileges are assigned using the `GRANT` command, which allows granting specific access privileges to users and roles within PostgreSQL.

Granting Privileges in PostgreSQL

To assign access privileges to users and roles in PostgreSQL, you can use the `GRANT` command, which allows granting specific access privileges to one or more users or roles. Access privileges allow defining the level of authorization and access rights to database objects, such as tables, views, stored procedures, and more.

For example, to grant the "administrator" role the read and write privilege on a table named "data," you can use the following SQL command:

```sql
GRANT SELECT, INSERT, UPDATE ON table data TO administrator;
```

Using the `GRANT` command, you can specify the access privileges you wish to grant, as well as the database objects on which to apply the privileges. Privileges can be assigned both at the level of individual objects and at the schema level, allowing precise definition of access control and permissions within the database.

Revoking Privileges in PostgreSQL

In addition to granting access privileges, you can revoke previously assigned privileges from users and roles using the `REVOKE` command, which allows selectively and customarily revoking access rights to database objects. Revoking privileges is an important operation to ensure the security and integrity of data within the database, limiting access to sensitive and critical resources.

For example, to revoke the read privilege on a table named "data" from the "administrator" role, you can use the following SQL command:

```sql
REVOKE SELECT ON table data FROM administrator;
```

Using the `REVOKE` command, you can revoke access privileges selectively and customarily, ensuring that only authorized users can access data and database resources. It is important to revoke privileges timely and accurately to avoid abuses and compromises to system security.

Best Practices for User and Privilege Management in PostgreSQL

To ensure proper management of users and privileges in PostgreSQL, it is important to follow some best practices and guidelines to ensure the security and integrity of data within the database. Below are some best practices to keep in mind during the configuration and management of access and permissions in PostgreSQL:

1. Use roles and groups to efficiently and securely organize and manage access privileges.

2. Limit access privileges to users and roles strictly necessary to perform their respective activities.

3. Periodically revoke unnecessary privileges and monitor access logs to identify suspicious activities.

4. Use encryption to protect sensitive and confidential data within the database.

5. Regularly back up data and privileges to ensure availability and integrity of stored information.

User and privilege management in

PostgreSQL is a crucial aspect to ensure the security and integrity of data within the database. By using the tools and techniques described in this guide, you can efficiently create and manage users, roles, and privileges, ensuring granular control over access and permissions within the system. By following recommended best practices and guidelines, you can effectively protect sensitive and confidential data, avoiding abuses and security compromises. With the proper configuration and management of users and privileges in PostgreSQL, you can ensure a secure and reliable database environment that supports business needs and ensures organizational operational continuity.

18.Creating Roles in PostgreSQL

Roles in PostgreSQL are essential to ensure data security and ensure that only authorized users can access sensitive information.

In this article, we will explore in detail how to create roles in PostgreSQL and how to assign them specific permissions to ensure proper access control.

What is a role in PostgreSQL?

In PostgreSQL, a role is a fundamental concept that defines the identity of a user or a group of users within the database. Roles can be associated with specific privileges that determine what operations can be performed within the database, which tables can be accessed, and what changes can be made to the information present.

There are two main types of roles in PostgreSQL: login roles and database roles. Login roles are associated with actual users accessing the database, while database roles are used to define permissions within the database itself.

Creating a role in PostgreSQL

To create a new role in PostgreSQL, you can use the `CREATE ROLE` command followed by the role name and any additional permissions. For example, to create a new role called "administrator" with the privilege to create new tables, you can use the following command:

```
```

CREATE ROLE administrator WITH CREATEDB;

```
```

This command will create a new role called "administrator" with the privilege to create new tables within the database. It is important to note that the `WITH CREATEDB` option grants the role the privilege to create new databases, which may not be necessary for all roles.

Assigning permissions to roles

After creating a role in PostgreSQL, you can assign specific permissions using the `GRANT` command. This command allows you to specify which privileges are granted to the role and on which objects within the database.

For example, to grant the "administrator" role the right to perform SELECT operations on the "customers" table, you can use the following command:

```
GRANT SELECT ON customers TO administrator;
```

This command will assign the "administrator" role the right to perform SELECT operations on the "customers" table, allowing them to view the information present in the table but not make changes to it.

Managing role permissions

It is important to carefully manage role permissions within PostgreSQL to ensure data security and prevent unauthorized access. You can use the `REVOKE` command to revoke specific permissions from a role or the `DROP ROLE` command to delete an existing role from the database.

For example, to revoke the right to perform SELECT operations on the "customers" table from the "administrator" role, you can use the following command:

```
```

REVOKE SELECT ON customers FROM administrator;

```
```

This command revokes the right to perform SELECT operations on the "customers" table from the "administrator" role, preventing them from viewing the information present in the table.

Default roles in PostgreSQL

PostgreSQL includes some default roles that are already present in the database and have default permissions assigned to them. Some common default roles include:

- `pg_read_all_settings`: has the right to read all database settings.

- `pg_read_all_stats`: has the right to read all database statistics.

- `pg_monitor`: has the right to monitor database activity.

You can assign these default roles to newly created roles using the `GRANT` command to ensure they have the appropriate permissions to perform desired operations.

Conclusions

Creating roles in PostgreSQL is a fundamental process to ensure data security and control access within the database. By using the `CREATE ROLE`, `GRANT`, `REVOKE`, and `DROP ROLE` commands, you can define roles with specific permissions and ensure that only authorized users can access sensitive information within the database.

Make sure to carefully manage role permissions and revoke any unnecessary privileges to ensure the database remains secure and protected from unauthorized access. With proper planning and role management, you can ensure data security and regulatory compliance within the PostgreSQL database.

19. Password Management in PostgreSQL

Password management in PostgreSQL is a fundamental aspect to ensure the security and integrity of the data contained within the database. Passwords are indeed one of the main protection systems used to limit unauthorized access to sensitive and confidential information.

PostgreSQL offers different ways to manage user passwords, allowing to configure custom security policies based on the specific needs of each organization. In this article, we will explore the various options available for password management in PostgreSQL, providing practical guidelines on how to implement them effectively and securely.

One of the key features of PostgreSQL for password management is the ability to define password complexity policies for users. This allows to enforce strict rules for creating passwords, such as minimum length, the presence of special characters, and the frequency of updates. In this way, it ensures that passwords are secure enough to resist common cyber attacks.

To configure a password complexity policy in PostgreSQL, you can use the pg_passwordcheck function, which allows to define desired parameters such as minimum length and the presence of special characters. Once the policy is defined, it can be associated with database users using the PASSWORD VALIDATION clause in the CREATE ROLE or ALTER ROLE statements.

For example, to define a password complexity policy that requires at least 8 characters, including one uppercase letter, one lowercase letter, one number, and one special character, you can execute the following SQL command:

```
```

CREATE POLICY pws_policy CHECK (pg_passwordcheck(password, 8, NULL, NULL, ")) IS NULL);

```
```

Once the policy is defined, it can be associated with a role using the PASSWORD VALIDATION clause:

```
```

CREATE ROLE my_role WITH LOGIN PASSWORD 'password' VALID UNTIL 'infinity' PASSWORD VALIDATION pws_policy;

```
```

This way, the user my_role can create a password that meets the criteria defined in the complexity policy, ensuring an adequate level of security for accessing the database.

In addition to defining password complexity policies, PostgreSQL also offers the ability to encrypt user passwords to protect them from unauthorized access attempts. To encrypt passwords, you can use the pgcrypto function, which allows generating MD5 or SHA-256 hashes from the plain-text password.

To encrypt a password using the SHA-256 algorithm, you can execute the following SQL command:

```
SELECT ENCODE(DIGEST('password', 'sha256'), 'hex');
```

Once you have the password hash, you can store it in the database using an update query on the pg_shadow table, which contains information about users and their encrypted passwords.

For example, to update the password of the user my_user with the SHA-256 hash of the password 'password123', you can execute the following SQL command:

```
```

UPDATE pg_shadow SET
usename='my_user',
passwd=ENCODE(DIGEST('password123',
'sha256'), 'hex') WHERE usename='my_user';

```
```

This way, the password of the user my_user will be encrypted using the SHA-256 algorithm, providing an additional level of security in case the pg_shadow table is compromised by a cyber attack.

Another important aspect of password management in PostgreSQL is the periodic rotation of passwords, which helps reduce the risk of long-term compromise due to a potential password breach by third parties. It is advisable to set password rotation policies that include regular expiration dates, forcing users to change their passwords regularly to maintain a high level of security.

To implement password rotation in PostgreSQL, you can use the password expiration feature, which allows defining an expiration date for user passwords. You can also configure the duration of the expiration using the PASSWORD EXPIRE clause, specifying the number of days within which the password must be changed by the user.

For example, to set a password rotation policy that requires users to change their passwords every 90 days, you can execute the following SQL command:

```

```

```
ALTER ROLE my_user PASSWORD
EXPIRE INTERVAL '90 days';
```

```

```

This way, the password of the user my_user will be considered expired after 90 days from its creation or last change, forcing the user to change it in order to access the database. This feature is particularly useful to ensure an adequate level of security over time, avoiding passwords remaining unchanged for extended periods and becoming vulnerable to potential attacks.

In addition to managing user passwords, PostgreSQL also offers the ability to configure access rules based on user roles and privileges, selectively limiting access to sensitive and confidential data in the database. By using PostgreSQL's access control features, you can define specific permissions for tables, columns, and operations allowed to users, ensuring granular control over information access.

For example, to grant the user my_user permission to read tables in the database without being able to modify them, you can execute the following SQL command:

```
```

GRANT SELECT ON ALL TABLES IN SCHEMA public TO my_user;

```
```

This way, the user my_user can run read

queries on tables in the database without being able to modify their content, providing an additional level of security compared to traditional password management.

Password management in PostgreSQL is a fundamental aspect to ensure the security and integrity of data within the database. By using the features of password complexity policies, encryption, rotation, and access control, you can implement an effective strategy to protect sensitive and confidential information from cyber attacks and security breaches. It is advisable to adopt a holistic approach to password management in PostgreSQL, combining different techniques and tools to ensure a level of security appropriate to the specific needs of each organization.

20. Use of extensions and creation of custom plugins in PostgreSQL

In PostgreSQL, there are extensions and custom plugins that allow users to extend the capabilities of the database to adapt to their specific needs.

Extensions are software packages that add extra functionality to PostgreSQL, allowing users to take advantage of new features without having to modify the database's source code. Extensions are designed to be modular and easy to install, enabling users to customize the database based on their specific requirements.

Custom plugins, on the other hand, are software components written by users themselves to extend the capabilities of PostgreSQL in a personalized way. Custom plugins enable users to create specialized features to solve specific problems or meet particular needs, offering a high degree of flexibility and control.

In this article, we will explore how to use extensions and create custom plugins in PostgreSQL, highlighting the benefits and potential of these advanced features to optimize the database's performance and tailor it to the user's specific needs.

Using extensions in PostgreSQL:

Extensions offer a wide range of additional features for PostgreSQL, allowing users to extend the capabilities of the database and improve performance. Some popular extensions include:

- PostGIS: an extension that adds geospatial functionality to PostgreSQL, enabling users to efficiently manage geographic data.

- pgcrypto: an extension that provides encryption functionality to ensure data security within the database.

- TimescaleDB: a specialized extension for storing and analyzing time-series data, ideal for efficiently managing temporal data.

- ddl_compare: an extension that allows users to compare database schemas and synchronize them easily and quickly.

- hstore: an extension that adds key-value storage functionality to the database, enabling users to efficiently manage unstructured data.

To use an extension in PostgreSQL, simply download it from the official repository and install it using the CREATE EXTENSION command. Once installed, the extension will be available for use within the database, allowing users to take advantage of the new features offered.

Creating custom plugins in PostgreSQL:

Custom plugins allow users to extend the capabilities of PostgreSQL in a personalized way, creating specialized features to meet specific needs. Custom plugins can be developed using the C programming language or other languages supported by PostgreSQL, such as PL/pgSQL or PL/Python.

Creating a custom plugin in PostgreSQL requires a good understanding of the database's internal workings and the APIs available for extension development. Custom plugins can be used to implement advanced features, such as custom compression algorithms, query optimizations, or new data types.

To create a custom plugin in PostgreSQL, follow these steps:

1. Define the plugin's objective: identify the problem to solve or the need to meet with the custom plugin.

2. Develop the plugin code: write the plugin code using the chosen programming language and following PostgreSQL's APIs and development guidelines.

3. Compile the plugin: compile the plugin code using the appropriate compilation tool for the chosen programming language.

4. Install the plugin: install the plugin within the PostgreSQL database using the CREATE EXTENSION command.

5. Test the plugin: verify the plugin's correct operation and address any issues encountered during testing.

Custom plugins offer users of PostgreSQL a high degree of flexibility and control, allowing them to create specialized features to optimize the database's performance and tailor it to their specific needs.

Conclusion:

Extensions and custom plugins offer PostgreSQL users the ability to extend the database's functionalities and create new features tailored to their specific needs. By using extensions and creating custom plugins, users can optimize the database's performance, improve data security, and efficiently manage specialized information.

PostgreSQL offers a wide range of advanced features for developing extensions and custom plugins, allowing users to fully exploit the database's capabilities and tailor it to their specific needs. With extensions and custom plugins, PostgreSQL continues to be a flexible and powerful solution for data management and manipulation, offering users the ability to customize the database in an advanced and innovative way.

21. Performance Monitoring in PostgreSQL

Performance monitoring in PostgreSQL is a crucial aspect to ensure that the database functions efficiently and optimally. PostgreSQL, one of the most popular relational databases in the world, offers various features and tools to monitor system performance and identify any issues that could affect the overall performance of the database. In this article, we will examine in detail the main tools and techniques used for performance monitoring in PostgreSQL, as well as best practices to follow to optimize the database's performance.

Performance Monitoring Tools in PostgreSQL

PostgreSQL offers several tools for monitoring the performance of the database, including:

1. **pg_stat_activity**: This system view provides detailed information on the ongoing activities in the database, including running queries, connected users, and information on active transactions. This tool is useful for monitoring active queries and identifying any blocking or resource locking issues.

2. **pg_stat_statements**: This PostgreSQL extension tracks statistics on queries executed in the database, including execution times, number of executions, and number of rows returned. This information is useful for identifying slow or inefficient queries and optimizing the database's performance.

3. **pg_stat_bgwriter**: This system view provides statistics on PostgreSQL's background writing process, including write rates, dirty buffers, and checkpoint information. This information is useful for monitoring the database's writing activity and identifying any performance issues related to data writing.

4. **pg_stat_replication**: This system view provides information on the state of data replication in PostgreSQL, including standby

states, replication latency, and WAL flow information. This tool is useful for monitoring the health and efficiency of data replication in a distributed database architecture.

5. **pg_monitor**: This PostgreSQL extension provides a range of additional monitoring for the database, including performance counters, status indicators, and advanced configuration options. This tool is useful for monitoring the database's performance in real-time and optimizing configuration settings to improve overall performance.

Performance Monitoring Techniques in PostgreSQL

In addition to the monitoring tools available in PostgreSQL, there are also several techniques and best practices that can be used to monitor and optimize the performance of the database, including:

1. **Monitoring query response times**:

Monitoring the response times of queries executed in the database is essential to identify slow or inefficient queries. Use tools like pg_stat_statements to track query execution times and optimize resource-intensive queries.

2. **Monitoring system resource usage**: Monitoring system resource usage, such as CPU, memory, and disk, is essential to ensure that the database functions efficiently. Use system monitoring tools like Nagios or Zabbix to track resource usage and identify any peaks or anomalies.

3. **Monitoring transaction locks**: Monitoring transaction locks is important to avoid resource blocking or deadlock situations in the database. Use tools like pg_locks and pg_stat_activity to identify conflicting transactions and resolve blocking issues promptly.

4. **Monitoring indexes and statistics**: Monitoring table indexes and statistics is crucial to ensure that queries are executed efficiently. Use tools like pg_stats and pg_index to analyze table statistics and

optimize indexes to improve query performance.

5. **Monitoring data replication**: Monitoring the state of data replication is important to ensure data consistency and integrity in a distributed database architecture. Use tools like pg_stat_replication to track the state of standby servers and monitor replication latency to identify any data synchronization issues.

Best Practices to Optimize Performance in PostgreSQL

In addition to using monitoring tools and the techniques described above, there are also several best practices that can be followed to optimize the performance of the database in PostgreSQL, including:

1. **Use indexes efficiently**: Using appropriate and optimized indexes for frequent queries is essential for ensuring optimal performance in the PostgreSQL

database. Analyze resource-intensive queries and add indexes to improve query performance.

2. **Use query execution plan cache**: Using the query execution plan cache to store execution plans of frequent queries is useful for improving database performance. Configure the size of the execution plan cache based on the database's needs and monitor cache usage to identify any query optimization issues.

3. **Properly configure shared memory**: Properly configuring shared memory in the PostgreSQL configuration file is essential for ensuring optimal database performance. Optimize shared memory settings, such as shared_buffers and work_mem, to adapt to the specific workload needs of the database and monitor memory usage to identify any resource allocation issues.

4. **Regularly monitor performance**: Regularly monitoring database performance is essential to identify any performance issues promptly and resolve them before they can negatively impact the overall system

performance. Schedule regular performance checks using system and performance monitoring tools to identify and resolve any performance issues in the database.

5. **Backup and optimize the database**: Regularly backing up the database and optimizing tables is crucial to improve overall system performance. Use tools like pg_dump to perform regular database backups and optimize tables using techniques such as index reconstitution and data reorganization to ensure optimal performance over time.

Conclusion

Performance monitoring in PostgreSQL is a

fundamental aspect to ensure that the database functions efficiently and optimally. By using the monitoring tools available in PostgreSQL, such as pg_stat_activity and pg_stat_statements, and following the techniques and best practices described above, it is possible to identify and promptly resolve any performance issues in the database and optimize the overall system performance. Regularly monitoring database performance, properly configuring memory settings, and using indexes efficiently are just some of the actions that can be taken to optimize database performance in PostgreSQL. By following these guidelines and using the recommended tools and techniques, it is possible to ensure optimal and reliable performance in the PostgreSQL database and maximize system performance over time.

22. Optimization of configurations in PostgreSQL

PostgreSQL is one of the most popular and widely used open source relational databases in the world. Its flexibility and power make it an ideal choice for many applications, but to ensure optimal performance, it is important to optimize PostgreSQL configurations based on the specific system requirements.

In this article, we will examine best practices for optimizing PostgreSQL configurations, to ensure high and stable performance for your applications. From essential configuration parameters to advanced optimization techniques, we will guide you through everything you need to get the most out of PostgreSQL.

Essential configuration parameters

Before delving into the details of advanced optimizations, it is important to understand some of the essential configuration parameters in PostgreSQL that can significantly impact database performance.

1. shared_buffers: This parameter determines the amount of memory allocated for data caching. It is important to allocate enough memory to this parameter to ensure that the database can cache frequently used data, reducing the number of disk reads and improving overall database performance.

2. work_mem: This parameter determines the amount of memory allocated for sorting and joining operations. Make sure to allocate enough memory to this parameter to avoid excessive disk usage during sorting and joining operations, which can significantly slow down database performance.

3. effective_cache_size: This parameter determines the estimated size of the operating system's data cache. It is important to configure this parameter correctly based on the available system memory, so that PostgreSQL can optimize data access strategies based on the availability of the operating system's cache.

4. max_connections: This parameter determines the maximum number of simultaneous connections allowed to the database. Make sure to configure this parameter correctly based on the expected database load, to avoid congestion and improve overall performance.

Advanced optimization techniques

In addition to essential configuration parameters, there are some advanced optimization techniques that can be used to further improve PostgreSQL performance.

Here are some of these techniques:

1. Partitioning: Data partitioning is an advanced technique that allows you to divide large tables into more manageable parts, improving query performance and reducing response time. By using partitioning, you can optimize data access and minimize the time required to perform search operations.

2. Query optimization: Another important technique for optimizing PostgreSQL performance is to optimize the queries themselves. By using appropriate indexes, avoiding costly operations like Cartesian joins, and limiting the number of columns returned in queries, you can significantly improve overall database performance.

3. Performance monitoring: Constantly monitoring database performance is essential to identify any issues or areas for improvement. By using performance

monitoring tools like pg_stat_statements and pg_stat_activity, you can identify slow queries, database locks, and other issues that may impact database performance.

4. Optimize server configuration: Make sure to properly configure the server on which PostgreSQL is running to achieve the best possible performance. This includes configuring memory, disks, and network settings optimally for the specific needs of the database.

Optimizing PostgreSQL configurations is essential to ensure high and stable performance for your applications. By using the essential configuration parameters and advanced optimization techniques described in this article, you can maximize database performance and ensure it can efficiently handle high workloads.

Always remember to constantly monitor

database performance and make any necessary improvements to ensure that PostgreSQL is operating at its best. With the right attention and care, you can achieve optimal performance from PostgreSQL and ensure your database runs smoothly for your applications.

23. Use of monitoring and diagnostic tools in PostgreSQL

PostgreSQL is one of the most popular relational databases in the world, used by many companies and organizations to efficiently and securely manage large amounts of data. But how can we ensure that our database is functioning correctly and that any problems are identified and resolved promptly? In this article, we will explore the use of monitoring and diagnostic tools in PostgreSQL, which allow us to monitor the performance of our database and identify any critical issues.

One of the main monitoring tools available for PostgreSQL is Pg_stat_statements, which provides detailed information on the queries executed on the database, including execution time, number of executions, and number of rows returned. This tool is particularly useful for identifying the slowest and most inefficient queries, which could impact the overall performance of the database. By using Pg_stat_statements, we can optimize our queries to make them more efficient and improve the database's performance.

Another important tool for performance monitoring in PostgreSQL is Pg_stat_activity, which provides information on the current activities on the database, including running processes, transaction status, and the time elapsed since the last query was executed. This tool helps us identify any blocks or concurrency issues that could cause slowdowns in the database, allowing us to intervene promptly to resolve them.

To monitor resource usage on the database server, we can use the Pg_stat_bgwriter tool, which provides information on the number of writes and reads performed by the PostgreSQL background process. This tool helps us identify any IO issues and optimize configuration settings to improve the database's performance.

To track performance over time and identify any recurring trends or issues, we can use external monitoring tools like Prometheus and Grafana, which allow us to create customized dashboards and visually display the performance metrics of our database clearly and intuitively. These tools allow us to monitor the database's performance in real-time and be immediately alerted in case of anomalies or critical issues.

In addition to performance monitoring, diagnosing issues in the database is also crucial. To identify and resolve any errors or malfunctions, we can use diagnostic tools like PgBadger, which analyzes PostgreSQL logs and provides detailed reports on activities and errors in the database. By using PgBadger, we can quickly identify any issues and intervene to resolve them before they impact the database's performance.

The use of monitoring and diagnostic tools is essential to ensure optimal performance and stability in our PostgreSQL database. Through the analysis of performance metrics and timely identification of issues, we can optimize our queries, improve configuration settings, and efficiently resolve malfunctions. Investing in monitoring and diagnosing our database is a crucial step to ensure an optimal user experience and maintain high standards of security and reliability in our information system.

24. Database Sharding Scalability in PostgreSQL

As workload and data to manage increase, it is essential for a database to scale efficiently to ensure high performance and support the growing needs of the application.

The concept of sharding has become increasingly popular in the database world as a method to improve scalability. Sharding is a data partitioning technique where the database is divided into smaller fragments called shards, which are distributed across separate servers. This allows for workload distribution and improved database performance, enabling the management of a much larger volume of data compared to a single database.

PostgreSQL is one of the world's most popular open-source relational databases and offers native support for scalability through sharding. In this guide, we will explore how to implement sharding scalability in PostgreSQL, its benefits, and best practices to ensure its success.

Sharding Strategies in PostgreSQL

There are several strategies to implement sharding in PostgreSQL, each with its own advantages and disadvantages. The most common strategies include:

- Range-based Sharding: in this approach, data is divided based on a specific range of values. For example, data can be divided based on creation date or a numerical field. This approach is useful when there is a high degree of data heterogeneity and queries often rely on specific value ranges.

- Hash-based Sharding: in this method, a hash of a data key is calculated and used to distribute data across shards. This approach is useful when evenly distributing data among shards is desired and there are no specific requirements for data distribution.

- List-based Sharding: in this approach, data is divided based on specific values of a field. For example, data can be divided based on users' city of residence. This approach is useful when controlling data placement on shards based on specific criteria is desired.

Each sharding strategy has its own advantages and disadvantages and may be suitable for different contexts depending on the application's needs and data to manage.

Benefits of Sharding Scalability in PostgreSQL

Implementing sharding scalability in PostgreSQL offers numerous benefits that can improve database performance and reliability, including:

- Better workload distribution: with data divided into separate shards on separate servers, workload can be distributed more evenly, ensuring high performance during peak usage.

- Increased storage capacity: by dividing data into separate shards, a much larger volume of data can be managed compared to a single database, enabling effective database scaling.

- Greater resilience: by distributing data across separate shards, the risk of data loss due to hardware errors or network issues can be reduced, ensuring greater database resilience.

- Horizontal scalability: by adding additional shards, the database can be horizontally scaled to handle an increasing number of users and data without compromising performance.

- Ease of management: PostgreSQL offers tools and native functionalities to support sharding, simplifying the management and maintenance of scalable databases.

Implementing Sharding Scalability in PostgreSQL

To implement sharding scalability in PostgreSQL, various approaches and tools available in the platform can be utilized. Some of the most common methods include:

- Using Foreign Data Wrappers: PostgreSQL offers support for Foreign Data Wrappers (FDW), allowing access to and management of data from external servers. FDWs can be used to create collections of shards and manage data distribution among shards.

- Using native partitioning: PostgreSQL provides native data partitioning functionality, allowing data to be divided based on specific criteria. Native partitioning can be used to create shards and distribute data effectively.

- Using extensions and libraries: there are numerous extensions and libraries available for PostgreSQL that enable sharding implementation and improve database scalability. For example, Citus Data offers a PostgreSQL extension that simplifies sharding scalability implementation.

Best Practices for Ensuring Sharding Scalability Success in PostgreSQL

To ensure the success of sharding scalability implementation in PostgreSQL, it is important to follow some best practices, including:

- Designing the sharding strategy: careful

planning of the sharding strategy is essential, taking into account application requirements, data distribution, and desired performance. Consider query requirements, database size, and data geographic distribution to ensure effective implementation.

- Performance monitoring: continuously monitor database performance and identify any issues or obstacles that may compromise scalability. Utilize performance monitoring tools to identify bottlenecks and optimize queries to improve performance.

- Backup and data recovery: regularly back up data and plan data recovery procedures in case of data loss or hardware issues. Maintain a backup copy of data on separate servers to ensure data security and availability.

- Load balancing: effectively manage load balancing among shards to ensure high performance and optimal workload support.

Utilize load balancing tools to monitor load on shards and distribute workload evenly across servers.

- Redundant data management: implement a data redundancy strategy to ensure continuous data availability in case of hardware failure or network issues. Use data replication on separate servers and plan failover procedures to ensure database operational continuity.

Conclusion

Sharding scalability is an effective method to improve performance and scalability of a PostgreSQL database, enabling the management of a much larger volume of data and users. By properly implementing sharding scalability and following best practices, effective implementation can be ensured to support the growing needs of the application.

PostgreSQL offers native support for sharding and a variety of tools and functionalities to simplify the implementation of scalable databases.

25.Data Replication and Database Clustering in PostgreSQL

Data replication and database clustering are two fundamental concepts in ensuring high availability, scalability, and reliability of a data management system like PostgreSQL. In this article, we will explore the various ways and techniques in which these concepts can be implemented in PostgreSQL.

Data Replication

Data replication is the process through which a database replicates data from one server to another. This allows for distributing data across multiple nodes, improving redundancy and system availability. PostgreSQL supports various approaches to data replication, including:

1. Asynchronous replication: in this approach,

data is replicated from a master server to one or more slave servers asynchronously. This means that the data is replicated at a later time compared to when it was modified on the master server. This approach is useful for improving the performance of the master server as there is no need to wait for the replication to complete before returning a confirmation to the user.

2. Synchronous replication: in this approach, data is replicated from a master server to one or more slave servers synchronously. This means that data modification on the master server is synchronized with the slave server before returning a confirmation to the user. This approach is useful for ensuring real-time data consistency across all nodes in the cluster.

3. Table-level replication: in this approach, it is possible to replicate only certain tables of a database instead of the entire database. This allows for optimizing data replication based

on specific system requirements.

4. Schema-level replication: in this approach, it is possible to replicate only certain schemas of a database instead of the entire database. This allows for separating different business logics on different nodes of the cluster.

Database Clustering

Database clustering is the process through which multiple instances of a database are managed on distinct physical or virtual nodes. This allows for distributing the workload across multiple nodes and ensuring high availability and scalability of the system. PostgreSQL supports various approaches to database clustering, including:

1. Two-node clustering: in this approach, two physical or virtual nodes are used to run two separate instances of PostgreSQL. This

increases redundancy and system availability.

2. Multi-node clustering: in this approach, multiple physical or virtual nodes are used to run multiple separate instances of PostgreSQL. This allows for distributing the workload across multiple nodes and ensuring greater system scalability.

3. Multi-node clustering: in this approach, a PostgreSQL database cluster is deployed across multiple physical or virtual nodes. This allows for managing large volumes of data and high-intensity workloads.

Implementing Data Replication and Database Clustering in PostgreSQL

To implement data replication and database clustering in PostgreSQL, various tools and technologies can be used, including:

1. Repmgr: Repmgr is an open-source tool that allows for managing database replication in PostgreSQL simply and efficiently. It can coordinate the configuration and management of master and slave servers as well as monitor the replication status.

2. Patroni: Patroni is an open-source tool that allows for managing database clustering in PostgreSQL simply and reliably. It can manage cluster node failover automatically and ensure data availability in case of failure.

3. Streaming replication: PostgreSQL supports the streaming replication mechanism to efficiently replicate data from a master server to one or more slave servers. This ensures high availability and system redundancy.

4. Logical replication: PostgreSQL supports the logical replication mechanism to flexibly and customizably replicate data from one server to another. This allows for replicating

only certain tables or schemas instead of the entire database.

Conclusion

Data replication and database clustering are essential concepts to ensure high availability, scalability, and reliability of a data management system like PostgreSQL. It is important to choose the most suitable approach for the system's needs and implement it correctly to avoid issues and ensure the system operates correctly. With the right tools and technologies, it is possible to implement data replication and database clustering effectively and efficiently in PostgreSQL.

26. Creating a web application using PostgreSQL

PostgreSQL is one of the most popular relational databases in the world, known for its reliability, scalability, and flexibility. With its powerful features, it is a great choice for developing complex web applications that require efficient data management. In this article, I will guide you through the necessary steps to create a web application using PostgreSQL as the main database.

Before getting started, make sure you have PostgreSQL installed on your server. You can download the latest version from https://www.postgresql.org/download/. Once installed, start the PostgreSQL service on your system and create a new database using the following command:

```sql
```

```
CREATE DATABASE your_database_name;
```
```

Once the database is created, you can start designing the database schema using SQL language. For example, let's imagine we need to create an application for managing an online library. We can start by defining the necessary tables to store information about books, authors, and users. Here is an example of how our database schema could look:

```sql
CREATE TABLE books (

    id SERIAL PRIMARY KEY,

    title VARCHAR(255),

    author_id INTEGER REFERENCES
authors(id),

    publication_year INTEGER

);
```
```

```
CREATE TABLE authors (

  id SERIAL PRIMARY KEY,

  first_name VARCHAR(100),

  last_name VARCHAR(100)
);


CREATE TABLE users (

  id SERIAL PRIMARY KEY,

  first_name VARCHAR(100),

  last_name VARCHAR(100),

  email VARCHAR(255)
);
```

Once the database schema is defined, we can start creating queries to interact with the data. PostgreSQL supports a wide range of data types and advanced functions, allowing us to write complex queries to meet the application logic. For example, to insert a book into the "books" table, we can use the following query:

```sql
INSERT INTO books (title, author_id, publication_year)
VALUES ('The Lord of the Rings', 1, 1954);
```

This query will insert a new book into the "books" table with the title "The Lord of the Rings", the author corresponding to id 1 (which we should have inserted previously in the "authors" table), and the publication year 1954.

Once we have defined our database schema and created the necessary queries to interact with the data, we can move on to creating the web application itself. For this exercise, we will use the Python programming language and the Flask web framework, along with the psycopg2 module for connecting to the PostgreSQL database.

Let's start by creating a new Python project and installing Flask and psycopg2 using the pip package manager. Make sure you have a virtual environment activated before installing the packages:

```
```

pip install Flask psycopg2

```
```

Once the packages are installed, we can start creating the web application. Create a new Python file called "app.py" and import the necessary libraries:

```python
from flask import Flask, render_template

import psycopg2
```

Next, define the connection information for the PostgreSQL database and establish a connection to the database in our code:

```python
conn = psycopg2.connect(
    dbname="your_database_name",
    user="your_user",
    password="your_password",
    host="localhost"
)

cur = conn.cursor()
```

```
```

Once the database connection is established, we can start defining the routes of the web application using Flask. For example, we can create a route to display all the books in the database:

```python
@app.route('/books')
def list_books():
    cur.execute("SELECT * FROM books")
    books = cur.fetchall()
    return render_template('books.html', books=books)
```

In this example, we used the cur.execute() function provided by psycopg2 to execute an SQL query that selects all the books in the "books" table. The results of the query are then passed to the "books.html" template along with the variable "books". Now let's add the code to render the template and display the books on the web page:

```html
<!DOCTYPE html>
<html lang="en">
<head>
    <meta charset="UTF-8">
    <meta http-equiv="X-UA-Compatible" content="IE=edge">
    <meta name="viewport" content="width=device-width, initial-scale=1.0">
    <title>List of books</title>
</head>
<body>
    <h1>List of books</h1>
```

```
<ul>

{% for book in books %}

    <li>{{ book[1] }} - {{ book[3] }}</li>

{% endfor %}

</ul>

</body>

</html>

```
```

In this template, we used the Jinja2 template engine of Flask to iterate over the query results and display the titles and publication years of the books. Of course, you can customize the template and add more information about the books according to the needs of the application.

Once the routes and templates of the application are defined, we can run the Flask application using the command:
```

```
```

```
flask run
```

```
```

Now the web application should be running locally on your server, allowing you to view and interact with the data in the PostgreSQL database. This is just a very simple example of creating a web application using PostgreSQL as the main database. With PostgreSQL and Flask, the possibilities are virtually limitless for developing complex and scalable web applications.

PostgreSQL is a powerful and versatile database that can be easily integrated into web development projects. With its advanced features and large community support, it is an excellent choice for developing robust and high-performance web applications.

27. Basic Syntax in PostgreSQL

Basic Syntax in PostgreSQL:

1. Creating a database:

To create a new database in PostgreSQL, you can use the SQL command CREATE DATABASE followed by the desired name for the database. For example:

CREATE DATABASE database_name;

2. Creating a table:

To create a new table within a PostgreSQL database, you can use the SQL command CREATE TABLE followed by the table name and the desired columns with their respective data types. For example:

CREATE TABLE table_name (

```sql
    id INT PRIMARY KEY,

    name VARCHAR(50),

    surname VARCHAR(50),

    age INT
);
```

3. Inserting data:

To insert new data into an existing table in PostgreSQL, you can use the SQL command INSERT INTO followed by the table name and the values to insert for each corresponding column. For example:

```sql
INSERT INTO table_name (id, name, surname, age)
VALUES (1, 'Mario', 'Rossi', 30);
```

4. Selecting data:

To select data from a table in PostgreSQL,

you can use the SQL command SELECT followed by the desired columns or '*' to select all columns. For example:

SELECT * FROM table_name;

5. Updating data:

To update existing data in a table in PostgreSQL, you can use the SQL command UPDATE followed by the table name and the values to update for each corresponding column, as well as any conditions to specify the records to update. For example:

UPDATE table_name

SET age = 35

WHERE id = 1;

6. Deleting data:

To delete data from a table in PostgreSQL,

you can use the SQL command DELETE followed by the table name and any conditions to specify the records to delete. For example:

```
DELETE FROM table_name

WHERE id = 1;
```

7. Dropping a table:

To drop an existing table in PostgreSQL, you can use the SQL command DROP TABLE followed by the table name to drop. For example:

```
DROP TABLE table_name;
```

These are just some examples of the basic syntax in PostgreSQL. The DBMS offers many other commands and advanced features for effective data management and complex query creation.

PostgreSQL Glossary:

1. Database: A database in PostgreSQL is an organized collection of structured data that can be stored, managed, and queried efficiently.

2. Table: A table in PostgreSQL is a structure that allows you to organize data in rows and columns for more efficient and structured management.

3. Column: A column in PostgreSQL is a single data unit within a table that represents a specific attribute for each record.

4. Row: A row in PostgreSQL is a single record within a table that contains values for each corresponding column.

5. Primary key: A primary key in PostgreSQL is a unique attribute within a table that uniquely identifies each record.

6. Foreign key: A foreign key in PostgreSQL is an attribute that establishes a relationship between two tables based on a common field.

7. JOIN: JOIN is an operator used in PostgreSQL to combine data from two or more tables based on a defined relationship between them.

8. Index: An index in PostgreSQL is a structure that enhances query performance by quickly identifying records within a table.

9. Transaction: A transaction in PostgreSQL is a set of operations that must be executed atomically and consistently to ensure data integrity.

10. Constraint: A constraint in PostgreSQL is a rule that defines validity conditions for the data within a table, such as primary and foreign keys.

This glossary provides an overview of the key words and concepts used in the context of PostgreSQL. With a thorough understanding of the syntax and basic features of this DBMS, you can effectively use PostgreSQL to manage and query data efficiently and reliably.

Index